The Meaning
of
Love

The Meaning of *Love*

New Insights

ALEXANDER EVANS JR

authorHOUSE®

AuthorHouse™
1663 Liberty Drive
Bloomington, IN 47403
www.authorhouse.com
Phone: 1-800-839-8640

Published by AuthorHouse   09/26/2012

ISBN: 978-1-4772-4387-9 (sc)
ISBN: 978-1-4772-4386-2 (e)

Library of Congress Control Number: 2012912424

DEDICATION

I'm dedicating this book to the human race, so that it may find the love that brings about peace on earth and brotherhood, and the meaning of love on a grander scale.

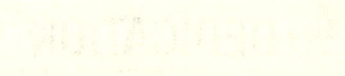

AUTHOR'S NOTES

The best way to read this book is not to read it at all, but to read each definition two or three times then take a minute, **think and reflect on the definition**. In some cases you will find that the more you read the definition, the more powerful the message about love is. One good way is to read it a definition a day, as this will so enrich the message profoundly and provide comfort to you throughout the day. This is the kind of book you will enjoy forever.

Love Quotes

*L*ove has nothing to
            do with "I" or "you". Love
       is about we or us.

*L*ove ensures that we
            not only becomes good but
       remain good people.

*L*ove's perfect because
            It is untouched by man kind
       but within all mankind.

*L*ove understands the
            challenges the heart encounters
       doing your lifetime.

*L*ove composes the theme
of millions of movies. But
much of its acting.

*L*ove brings all human
beings to live to their highest
potential on Earth.

*L*ove understands the
great wisdom within us all
as children of God.

*L*ove brings to us the
highest human conditions that
permits peace on earth.

*L*ove, achieves wisdom;
      It's the very foundation
of all human knowledge.

*L*ove, increases your brain
      power and reasoning; with
      no insecurity.

*L*ove requires your
      attention, communication,
and sharing yourself.

*L*ove maintains itself
      grows by itself for the
      sake of creation.

*L*ove achieves an almost
  mystical sense, and can take
  many other forms.

*L*ove will operate
  apart from the mind, when wild
  passions awaken.

*L*ove demonstrates the
  depth and breadth, of God's love
  for us the human race.

*L*ove appreciates
  and is grateful, but lust is
  not aware of such.

*L*ove will cause divine
justice to be tempered with
mercy and goodness.

*L*ove demonstrates clearly
that justice, and love, are the
keys that open Doors.

*L*ove eliminates
hate, with goodness beyond man's
true understanding.

*L*ove demonstrates grace.
It pursues truth, justice and
peace around the world.

*L*ove enlightens us.
        It effectively triumphs
    over ignorance.

*L*ove cooperated then
        God said, "Let us make man
    in our own likeness.

*L*ove, emphasizes
            our commonalities, a
    bridge across the gap.

*L*ove emphasizes
            having joy as often as
    you possibly can.

*L*ove improves attitude,
relationships, and the wide
perception of life.

*L*ove integrates but
hatred disintegrates it. Love
gives power strength.

*L*ove absolutely
everything else profits you
nothing, after death.

*L*ove repairs broken
hearts, elevates souls, restores and
heals hurtful places.

*L*ove cooperates with
    God's work to lift humankind
    out of its wet mud.

*L*ove separates you
    and allows, you to live as
a whole complete being

*L*ove intensifies the
    natural joys of life, when
    we love each other.

*L*ove goes a very
    long way when you reflect on
    its spiritual scope.

*L*ove can help us know
what everlasting life is
right now and right here.

*L*ove finds a way so
it can change your darkest days
into your brightest.

*L*ove with logic does
provides world and self-knowledge
for daily living.

*L*ove for yourself is
the key that develops your own
great spiritual strength.

*L*ove gives people
      the ability to love
   the unlovable.

*L*ove enlightens the
      consciousness with divine
   insights and truth.

*L*ove assures that fear
      departs and faith endures as
   hurts renew themselves.

*L*ove's needs are no
      different than yours, except
   it's not obvious.

*L*ove emphasizes
    strong feelings deep attachment
        to life's emotions.

*L*ove enlightens the
        consciousness gives divine
        insights and truth.

*L*ove broadens visions
        and perspectives and opens
        doors of great wisdom

*L*ove looks for certain
        qualities in human beings
        like devotion to God.

*L*ove demonstrates grace
  It pursues truth, and justice,
  across all cultures.

*L*ove will broaden your
  focus and your horizons
  of truth and justice.

*L*ove detects all the
  pitfalls and finds a safe place
  for you to take rest.

*L*ove adds a deeper
  dimension to living life
  found within yourself.

*L*ove alerts us to
the grim facts of evil men
goodness tells its truth.

*L*ove adapts to the
changes within relationships based
on goodness and truth.

*L*ove accomplishes
what it set out to do; it
creates more people.

*L*ove is the supreme
answer for all mankind which
waits for peace on earth.

*L*ove wants to be your
　　　life; it wants to rescue you
　　from a living hell.

*L*ove forces you to
　　　open up and realize that
　　truth itself means life.

*L*ove begins by
　　　noticing the lovable
　　within all people.

*L*ove understands the
　　　mysteries of life. Where we
　　come from and go too.

*L*oves opens its self
    exposes its self, places its self
deep in the heart's life.

*L*ove touches us all
    no matter who we are where
we are, He loves you.

*L*ove defends all and
    believes all, hopes all, bears all;
He's never exhausted.

*L*ove confirms His own
    fundamental conscientiousness
in all human beings.

*L*ove achieves a real
result that overturns logic
place time and all thought.

*L*ove gives all a chance
to catch a glimpse of sacred
wisdom in God's mind.

*L*ove knows nothing of
the ego. Its expression starts
within the heart.

*L*ove understands all the
mysteries, whereof we came
and whereto we go!

*L*ove gives us some of
the greatest insights
into God own heart.

*L*ove requires you to
explore deeper stages of life
from within your heart.

*L*ove ultimately
comes from forgiveness, the path
to peace and to truth.

*L*ove will reveal the
transforming power of truth
as compassion.

*W*hen God is present
within that's when you'll find that
love will never end.

*L*ove requires effort
love never dies, but only
gets greater with time.

*L*ove, requires change
and helps many people to
grow in righteousness.

*L*ove wants to share with
you the mysteries and wonders
of all creation.

*R*eal love becomes more
complex, intellectual,
imaginative.

*L*ove and justice a
theology for truth and
moral revival.

*L*ove wants only the
reunion to itself, that
is found within you.

*L*ove accomplishes
feats far more wonderful than
all the stars you see.

*L*ove feels the same
    way as you feel and others feel—
  love feels like God feels.

*L*ove eliminates
    the distance between God and
    His people on earth.

*L*ove wants to share with
    you the mysteries and great wonders
    of all great creation.

*L*ove is the life of
    all mankind, it gives itself
    to you forever.

*L*ove as if the act
itself will never end, make
love feel forever.

*L*ove maintains itself
grows within you with every
beat within your heart.

*L*ove has nothing to
do with what you expect but
what's expected of you.

*L*ove keeps you from being
full of yourself keeps you humble.
so you know yourself.

*L*ove requires us to
explore the inner part of
our own minds for truth.

*L*ove activates your
intrinsic powers, which are
otherwise dormant.

*L*ove keeps on loving
when hate is everywhere as
evil hides from light.

*L*ove requires acts
of goodness toward others
as well as yourself.

*L*ove creates an
     environment in which you
  can cherish your life.

*L*ove captures the heart
     in a second and then holds on
     for forever.

*L*ove brings the depth of
     passion wisdom which is
    essential to life.

*L*ove satisfies the senses
     and spiritual needs of
  lovers and much more.

*L*ove enlightens our
knowledge of ourselves so we
experience life's joys.

*L*ove gives you the strength
to endure the ultimate
journey living life.

*L*ove crosses the shores
of death itself when you are
remembered by friends.

*L*ove wants to be born
again within you making
you its own temple.

*L*ove looks for people
upon whom it can shower
itself forever.

*L*ove ultimately
brings us beyond pain and
sorrow to happiness.

*L*ove ensures that we
not only become sinless
but become perfect.

*L*ove accomplishes
God's purposes in our world.
to show the whole truth.

*L*ove brings the depth,
　　　　passion and wisdom that
changes the whole world.

*L*ove a power which
　　　works within us constantly
perfecting each one.

*L*ove explains the great
　　　miracle of children, as
a sign of God's love.

*L*ove "Hurts", when couples
　　　talk less and care less about
each other's feelings.

*L*ove defends us it
      makes every effort to keep
   you from evil things.

*L*ove fades when lies are
      told and accepted as truth
   by most good people.

*L*ove looks for the day
      when all mankind seeks peace
      and togetherness.

*L*ove God supremely
      and serve Him within your own
   heart for a lifetime.

*L*ove wants to be your
      friend it wants to save you from
      living in hell on earth.

*L*ove and justice as
        a theology will lead to
      peace in all mankind.

*L*ove knows itself and
     it knows you, mankind, and God
     it knows of all things.

*L*ove achieves the deed
       of turning silence into
     emotional thought.

*L*ove reveals itself
        as the matchless level of
    all understanding.

*L*ove alerts us to
        one another. We are not just
    lonely scattered souls.

*L*ove wants you to know
        this, you are pre-approved
    and qualified for life.

*L*ove defends you and
        makes every effort to keep
    you out of danger.

*L*ove clarifies your
        vision of complexities
    makes this life simple.

*L*ove gives you the full
      freedom to confess, that you
    were wrong and sorry.

*L*ove requires that
      all be cared for and none
    go without essentials.

*L*ove the greatest of
      all blessings to mankind from
    mankind's creator

*L*ove requires you to
practice justice—with love and
truth, in return peace!

*L*ove achieves the real
results that sometimes overturn
logic and the truth.

*L*ove looks for common
ground so it flourishes and
grow from deep within.

*Y*ou can't be loved
if you don't love yourself first.
First you then others.

*L*ove satisfies the most
important of all needs: the
need to love others.

*L*ove "The Salvation"
for mankind is completed
in one human being.

*L*ove yourself and as
a result you will know your
own self's respect.

*L*ove knows how to keep
you alive inside outside
and beyond the earth.

*L*ove clarifies truth
  and makes life's complexities
  a lot like child-play.

*L*ove broadens and it
  deepens in such a way life
  becomes a movie.

*L*ove articulates
  what's in the heart without
  fear of saying it.

*L*ove comes in countless
  forms it's expressed in dance, song,
speech, touch and right now!

*L*ove authorizes
you to voice that which is in
your own deepest truths.

*L*ove will not defend
itself. You are to defend
its right to exist.

*L*ove activates the
unseen bonds between you, God
and all of mankind.

*L*ove created you
and provided you its life
wonder and beauty.

The object of love
        to show you the truth within
        your very own heart.

The strength of love
                Is to bring integrity
        and truth to mankind.

Love accomplishes
        amazing things when good things
                are done for others.

Love is the supreme
                answer for all the problems
        of mankind for good.

*L*ove created me
    it loves me, and passes through
        me into others.

*L*ove confirms God's own
    fundamental conscientiousness
        living within all.

*L*ove forever will
    endure, Faith will be eternal
        within you always.

*L*ove keeps us going
        It's the fuel to the sacred
    fire that's in mankind.

*L*ove ensures us that
we will never be alone
while loving others.

*L*ove gives you space to
be yourself in the light of
others around you.

*L*ove establishes
a sense of unity through words
understanding all.

*L*ove authorizes
people to consider what
can be done different.

*L*ove activates the
     unseen bond between you God
     and the human race.

*L*oves meditations
     are sadness, pain, humor
     joy and happiness.

*L*ove means to be the
     playground for love ones to
     express their feeling.

*L*ove, requires change
     that facilitate others to
     grow in righteousness.

*L*ove forces you to
open up and realize that
the truth is better.

*L*ove requires your
perception, emotions, words
thoughtfulness to work.

*L*ove proves the existence
of God is true, and you know
it's about your heart!

*L*ove gives you some of
the greatest insights into
heaven and of hell.

*L*ove wants to break down
        the boundaries that are set
        that to divide us.

*L*ove gives all people
        liberty which makes people
        free and equal beings.

*L*ove gives all a sense
            of unity with all of
            human creation.

*L*ove gives you the strength
            to demand justice for all and
    stand strong against evil.

*L*ove real truths are
　　　often found in the hearts
　　of those impoverish.

*L*ove looks for people
　　　upon whom it can shower
　　grace and joy for life.

*L*ove will never grow
　　　old; love will never die. Love
　　will always stay truth.

*L*ove starts with you
　　　noticing the lovable
　　in others like you.

*L*ove begins with an
      effort to making what is
wrong to what is right.

*L*ove begins with a
      recognition of God's love
in all human being.

*L*ove thinks of mankind
      as free self-determined souls
with choices and chances.

*L*ove accomplishes
      amazing things that keeps all
earth people alive.

*L*ove awakes from within
　　　it whispers to your heart and
　　then changes your mind.

*L*ove enlightens and
　　　elevates consciousness with
　　great divine insight.

*L*ove forgives all things
　　　it does not repose in
　　your forgiveness.

*I*f you don't understand
　　　love You don't understand any
　　thing about living.

*L*ove runs deeper than
romantic fascination
and physical gifts.

*L*ove touches everyone
no matter who they are, or
what they are in life.

*L*ove wants to be loved
as you want to be loved
you get the best thought.

*L*ove is what sustains
you through all of the hard and
the difficult times.

*L*ove looks for people
who want to succeed over
come lies in this world.

*L*ove broadens each day.
You can't go wrong with it.
Your heart will thank you.

*L*ove broadens your own
vision for others' perspective
and your peace of mind.

*L*ove can be found all
around us. One profound truth
after each new moment.

*L*ove confirms your own
         basic responsibility
  a good human being.

*L*ove creates justice
   and righteousness so people can
     become intelligence.

*L*ove gives us a chance
    to catch a glimpse of sacred
  wisdom in God's mind.

*L*ove sees clearly and
   accepts your faults and doesn't
   hold it against you.

*L*ove created and
      provided you the means to
your own redemption.

*L*ove yourself and you
      are bound to hear someone say
one day I love you.

*L*ove can
      conclude arguments and end
all contradictions.

*L*ove requires as its
      groundwork the cultivation
of truth with in you.

*L*ove will never die
　　　it wipes a away your tears
　　refreshes your soul.

*L*ove composes the key
　　　elements, that makes a life
　　solid understanding.

*L*ove the salvation
　　　for a lost world is possible
　　not Impossible.

*L*ove wants to be your
　　　your God and live within you
　　now and forever.

*L*ove wants pure justice
in the world, so that none are
better than another.

*L*ove causes us to see
people not as "others" but
as a family.

*L*ove a corrective
force that brings all people
true understanding.

*L*ove comes to you as
ordinary truth; you can
find comfort in it.

*L*ove keeps the whole world
    from going mad prevents hate
  war and destruction.

*L*ove the emotion
    that is based on what the heart
  feels and comprehends.

*L*ove achieves your own
    journey in life, awakening
  you to your present.

*L*ove assures us that
    divine empathy extends
  not only to earth.

*L*ove revitalizes
you and helps your relationship
to thrive with the truth.

*L*ove eliminates
deception and distrust and
restores our truth.

*L*ove begins with self
acceptance and forgiveness
of your own self.

*L*ove satisfies in
a way that erotic love
can never create.

*L*ove demonstrates grace.
It pursues truth, and justice,
across all cultures.

*L*ove emphasize
strong feelings deep attachment,
and a commitment.

*L*ove achieves a kind
of transcendence for all of
those who love God.

*L*ove reveals what women
need to know about the male
ego and his ways.

*L*ove establishes a
communion with people
through their relationships.

*L*ove appears complex
ambiguous to the those
most educated.

*L*ove understands the art
of transforming the human
beings into spirits.

*L*ove understands that
no relationship succeeds
without forgiveness.

*L*ove gives wings to the
heart steps to the words that
move you to action.

*L*ove isn't about
changing people it's about
excepting the changes.

*T*he deepest love is
expressed without words but
felt within your heart.

*L*ove must be as free
as an eagle's wing hovering
over the lands and sea.

*L*ove enlightens minds
　　　and gives wisdom like, That of
Moses, Christ, and Buddha.

*L*ove keeps you going
　　　It's the fuel to a sacred
　　fire within you.

*L*ove ensures that you
　　　will continue to exist on
　　this earth after death.

*L*ove is for One God
　　　One Heaven, One Earth and one
　　people living on earth.

*L*ove activates The
      Unseen bonds between you and
      your own Creator.

*L*ove articulates
         its preferences in the
      hearts of all man kind.

*L*ove articulates
    the words that come from your mouth
      found within the heart.

*L*ove empowers
    you to say what's in your own heart
      without fear or.

*L*ove ultimately
　　lives for forgiveness, which is
　　the path to freedom.

*L*ove: the greatest of
　　all blessings that God has
　　given to His People.

*L*ove articulate,
　　the profound emotions
　　found
　　in all human beings.

*L*ove-The incurable
　　condition that ought to be
taught in your new schools.

*L*ove, it's your choice—
　　　Not a feeling or emotion
　　but your decision.

*L*ove is visible
　　　it's in everything you feel
　　touch, Taste, hear, and see.

*L*ove defines who we
　　　are and gives each of us its
　　own identity.

*L*ove activates the
　　　many emotional levels
　　from in our own heart.

*L*ove activates an
        intrinsic power which is
    otherwise your own.

*L*ove activates the
        inner heart within and makes
            it creation.

*L*ove operates under
            its own principle not
        only Romantic.

*L*ove establishes
            a trust and unity with
        self-understanding.

$\mathcal{L}$ove can achieve a
    quieting place in yourself
    a deeper partner.

Notes and Reflections

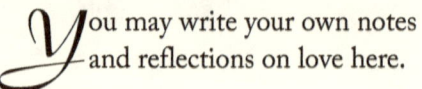
*Y*ou may write your own notes and reflections on love here.

_____

_____

_____

_____

_____

_____

_____

_____

_____

_____

_____

_____

_____

_____

_____

_____

_____

_____

_____

_____

_____

_____

_____

_____

_____

_____

_____

_____

_____

_____

$\mathcal{Y}$ou may write your own notes
and reflections on love here.

_____
_____
_____
_____
_____
_____
_____
_____
_____
_____
_____
_____
_____
_____
_____
_____
_____
_____
_____
_____
_____
_____
_____
_____
_____

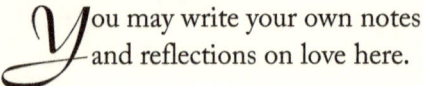

You may write your own notes
and reflections on love here.

_____

_____
_____
_____
_____
_____
_____
_____
_____
_____
_____
_____
_____
_____
_____
_____
_____
_____
_____
_____
_____
_____
_____
_____
_____
_____
_____
_____
_____
_____
_____
_____
_____

*Y*ou may write your own notes
and reflections on love here.

_____

_____
_____
_____
_____
_____
_____
_____
_____
_____
_____
_____
_____
_____
_____
_____
_____
_____
_____
_____
_____
_____
_____
_____
_____
_____
_____
_____
_____
_____
_____
_____
_____

If you read this book over and over
you will find each time you complete
it you will have a greater sense
of what love is, what it feels like
and what to do about it. Your sense
of love will definitely deepen
and become more profound.

Special notice
If you would like to get personalized
autographed copy of this book
the cost is $20 and a dollar
for postage. Send check to Evans
Evans PO Box 53, Brooklyn, NY 11235